I'M A PSYCHOLOGIST

LAUREN KUKLA

ILLUSTRATED BY **TOM HEARD**

MAYO CLINIC PRESS KIDS

With gratitude to Emily A. McTate, PhD

MAYO CLINIC PRESS KIDS | An imprint of Mayo Clinic Press
200 First St. SW
Rochester, MN 55905
mcpress.mayoclinic.org

To stay informed about Mayo Clinic Press, please subscribe to our free e-newsletter at mcpress.mayoclinic.org or follow us on social media.

For bulk sales contact Mayo Clinic at SpecialSalesMayoBooks@mayo.edu.

Proceeds from the sale of every book benefit important medical research and education at Mayo Clinic.

ISBN: 9798887701141 (paperback) | 9798887701134 (library binding) | 9798887701554 (ebook) | 9798887701257 (multiuser PDF) | 9798887701158 (multiuser ePub)

Library of Congress Control Number: 2023024579
Library of Congress Cataloging-in-Publication Data is available upon request.

TABLE OF CONTENTS

CHAPTER 1

HELLO!

Hello! My name is Rosa Perez. At work, my patients call me Dr. Rosie. I'm a child psychologist!

A psychologist is a doctor or healthcare provider. But I don't look in my patients' ears or throats. I focus on what my patients are thinking and feeling.

Psychologists work in many places. Most work at **clinics**. Some work at hospitals. I work at a **pediatric** clinic.

Clinic

I help kids manage thoughts, feelings, and behaviors. It's normal for kids to have fears and worries. I help my patients learn to deal with them.

CHAPTER 2

A PSYCHOLOGIST'S TOOLS & TEAM

Being a psychologist takes special skills. We need to be **empathetic** and curious. We also need to be good listeners.

There are a few tools that help me do my job. I take notes using a clipboard, pen, and paper. I don't write down everything my patients say. But I write enough so I can remember the visit later.

I work with other members of my healthcare team to care for patients. **Meet some of the people on the team!**

HANNAH
RECEPTIONIST
Schedules appointments

ALEX

NURSE

Gathers information from patients, answers questions, and gives **vaccines**

DR. MELNIK

PEDIATRICIAN

Provides medical care to patients

CHAPTER 3

A DAY AS A PSYCHOLOGIST

My day starts bright and early! It's a nice day, so I bike to work.

At the clinic, I look over my list of today's patients. I read why they are coming to see me. I look at their medical histories. Then, Alex tells me my first patient is ready!

7:35 AM

Lucy's family just moved here from another city.

"Lucy, I understand you're at a new school this year," I say. "What's it like?"

Lucy is quiet, so I suggest we play a game. After a few minutes, Lucy tells me she misses her old school.

13

8:30 AM

Lukas has trouble paying attention in school. He is falling asleep in class.

"We all have things in life that can be stressful," I say. "What are some of the things in your life that are stressful right now?"

Lukas tells me his parents are getting a **divorce**.

"I'm so sorry," I say. "Let's talk more about that."

9:45 AM

Otis has been acting out at school.

"Every feeling is okay," I say. "But not every action is allowed."

Otis, his dad, and I come up with a plan for how Otis can manage big feelings.

11:00 AM

Ada goes to her school nurse's office every day with a tummy ache. But Dr. Melnik doesn't think Ada is sick. I talk to Ada and her mom. The tummy aches started on her first day of kindergarten. I think Ada has **anxiety** about school that is causing her tummy aches.

17

Izzy is nervous about getting her flu shot. Izzy and I make a plan for how the poke will go. She gets to choose which arm she wants the vaccine in. Izzy wants Alex to count to three before giving her the shot. She also wants to hold her mom's hand during the shot.

2:15
PM

Kat has been having big feelings. She draws while we talk.

"I get really mad sometimes," Kat says.

"Feelings are like the weather," I say. "They can be strong. But they don't last forever."

3:30 PM

Advik has trouble falling asleep at night. We talk about worries that might be keeping Advik awake. We practice breathing exercises. Advik can do these right before bed.

Leo has a new baby sister. Since she was born, he's been having **tantrums**.

I give Leo some toy dinosaurs to play with. I ask him what he likes and doesn't like about being a big brother.

While Leo plays, I talk to his parents about how to support him.

4:45 PM

During every **session**, I take notes. Near the end of the day, I type up the notes on my computer.

CHAPTER 4

PATIENTS COME FIRST

Esme is my last patient of the day. We have a video visit. Esme is thirteen. She has been my patient since she was seven years old!

We talk about what's going on in Esme's life. She tells me she has been worried about speaking up in class. We make a plan for Esme to practice things she might say so it won't be so scary.

Being a psychologist isn't always easy. There aren't always enough **mental health** resources for kids who need them. It can be hard to get my patients the care they need.

Still, I love my job. It's an honor to get to know my patients and their families. At the end of the day, I know that I've helped my patients.

REAL-LIFE HERO!

MEET A REAL-LIFE PSYCHOLOGIST!

NAME: Dr. Emily McTate

JOB: Pediatric Psychologist

PLACE OF WORK: Mayo Clinic

What is your favorite part of being a psychologist?

I really enjoy getting to know patients and families. It is a privilege. I'm honored to be able to help patients and families make changes that improve their coping.

What does a psychologist do?

I learn about the patients and their families. I work with my patients to identify what they want help with and what's most important to them. Then I come up with some ideas to help them feel better. For example, if a patient is struggling with anxiety, we might practice doing some of the things that make them nervous.

What is the hardest part about being a psychologist?

I know there are more kids who need services than we have psychologists, counselors, or therapists to help them. I also don't like writing notes!

What character traits do you think it's important for psychologists to have?

Psychologists need to be curious and caring. It's also important to be a good listener. Psychologists need to be **flexible**. We never know what a patient is going to need help with!

CURIOSITY

Health heroes have special superpowers that help them do their jobs. One of a psychologist's most important superpowers is curiosity! I ask questions about my patients and their lives. I listen carefully to what a patient is telling me. By being curious, I can provide my patients the best care possible.

HOW DO YOU SHOW CURIOSITY IN YOUR LIFE?

GLOSSARY

anxiety—feelings of worry or nervousness

clinic—a healthcare building where patients have scheduled visits with healthcare providers

divorce—a legal end of a marriage

empathetic—able to relate to a person's feelings and understand what they're going through

flexible—able to change plans or actions quickly in different situations

mental health—a person's well-being in their emotions, thoughts, and relationships. Mental health is about how a person thinks, feels, and behaves.

pediatric—relating to healthcare for young people

session—a meeting or period of time when a certain activity takes place

tantrum—an emotional outburst expressing anger and frustration

vaccine—a drug that helps the body prepare an immune response against a certain germ to prevent disease

LEARN MORE

Kinder, Wynne. *Calm: Mindfulness for Kids*. New York: DK Publishing, 2019.

Nemours KidsHealth. "Going to a Therapist." https://kidshealth.org/en/kids/going-to-therapist.html

Psychology.org. "A Day in the Life: Clinical Psychologist Dr. Kezia Jackson." https://www.psychology.org/resources/day-in-the-life-clinical-psychologist/

Winters, Erin. *When a Donut Goes to Therapy*. Snowfall Publications, 2022.

Wonderopolis. "What Is Mental Health?" https://wonderopolis.org/wonder/What-Is-Mental-Health

INDEX